Man Your Gates

You Hold the Gate Key

Wale Akinosun

A GOSHEN PUBLISHERS BOOK VIRGINIA

Man Your Gates
You Hold the Gate Key

ISBN: 978-1-7370949-7-5

Library of Congress Cataloging-in-Publication Data

Published in 2023 by:

GOSHEN PUBLISHERS LLC
P.O. Box 1562
Stephens City, Virginia, USA
www.GoshenPublishers.com

Our books may be purchased in bulk for promotional, educational, or business use. For inquiries, please contact the publisher via email: Agents@GoshenPublishers.com.

First Edition 2023

Cover designed by Goshen Publishers LLC

Printed in the United States of America

All scriptures are quoted from the New King James Version of the Bible unless otherwise noted.

Dedication

This book is dedicated to the members of Schaumburg Community Church.

May you be connected, encouraged, and empowered to fulf ll your Godly responsibilities within your homes and community.

Contents

I. Introduction

Gated communities are not new. There are articles that suggest that they began in England in the nineteenth century. Many think that the first one found in America was in that same timeframe. These communities are exclusive to the people who live there and are separated from neighboring communities with walls and gates.

But, did you know there were gated communities in the Old Testament?

When Nebuchadnezzar had destroyed the Jewish temple, Ezra concerned himself with rebuilding it. Cyrus, the King of Persia, issued a decree permitting the Jews to return to Jerusalem after seventy years of captivity. This was a crucial moment in history. The Israelites who returned were rebuilding. Their work was repeatedly hampered by shortages of resources and external opposition. The people become so discouraged that God sent the prophets Haggai and Zechariah to encourage them. They finally completed and dedicated the temple. To protect it, they also built a wall around Jerusalem and erected gates to control access.

Twelve years later, Jerusalem was in shambles again, both physically and spiritually. Nehemiah went to inspect the damage. He found that the wall had been broken down and the gates had been burned.

How does that happen? That is what this book is about. According to scripture, your body is a temple where the Holy Spirit resides (1 Cor 6:19). By the end of this book, you will be equipped to *Man Your Gates*.

II. Shake It Off

When Jesus taught the disciples how to pray, He emphasized consecration ("Thy will be done"), universality ("in earth"), and conformity ("as it is in heaven"). Have you ever imagined what it is like to be really useful to the Lord? To devote all your talents to Him? To remain diligent even when your destiny is delayed?

David had been anointed king long before he was appointed to possess the throne of Israel. Using that as just one example, we can be confident that God's counsels will always be fulfilled despite any difficulties or delays that arise, and that they are always timely.

David's Lessons

During David's seven years and six-month reign over Judah, he led them to many victories (1 Sam 17:1–18:30). It is no wonder then that when all of Israel saw Saul was dead, and the other tribes beside Judah had no king, they gathered to make David king and unite the nation again under him.

1 Then all Israel came together to David at Hebron, saying, "Indeed we are your bone and your flesh.

2 Also, in time past, even when Saul was king, you were the one who led Israel out and brought them in; and the Lord your God said to you, 'You shall shepherd My people Israel, and be ruler over My people Israel.'"

3 Therefore all the elders of Israel came to the king at Hebron, and David made a covenant with them at Hebron before the Lord. And they anointed David king over Israel, according to the word of the Lord by Samuel.

4 And David and all Israel went to Jerusalem, which is Jebus, where the Jebusites were, the inhabitants of the land.

5 But the inhabitants of Jebus said to David, "You shall not come in here!" Nevertheless David took the stronghold of Zion (that is, the City of David).

(1 Chr 11:1–5)

9 So David went on and became great, and the Lord of hosts was with him.

10 Now these were the heads of the mighty men whom David had, who strengthened themselves with him in his kingdom, with all Israel, to make him king, according to the word of the Lord concerning Israel.

11 And this is the number of the mighty men whom David had: Jashobeam the son of a Hachmonite, chief of the captains;

he had lifted up his spear against three hundred, killed by him at one time.

(1 Chr 11:9–11)

How long do you wait for a promise? How do you not lose hope? Those questions we ask now are the same that those before us have asked. Even in biblical days, human nature led us to those same concerns. David had been anointed as king many years prior, when he was just fifteen years old. By the time they came to ordain him as king, he was thirty. To David, that fifteen years of waiting was a long time. To date, it was half of his life.

I imagine there has been a time in your life, perhaps even now, when you've had to wait, and it almost feels like you've been forgotten. Maybe you even feel like the day will never come that your promise is fulfilled. But I assure you, God's promises are always fulfilled. Scriptures tell us that more than once.

Hope deferred makes the heart sick, but when the desire comes, it is a tree of life.

(Pro 13:12)

Wait on the Lord; be of good courage, and He shall strengthen your heart; wait, I say, on the Lord!

(Ps 27:14)

At the time, they were just then realizing that David was God's chosen man for the kingdom. If David were alive today, we would be giving thanks to him for sharing his testimony. Fifteen years was a long time to wait, and he is an example of patience.

But what of David's other characteristics? Let us examine what else made David so successful.

David Was Not Afraid to Fail

David took chances that many people would not take. When he had opportunities to kill Saul, he did not do so.

1 Now it happened, when Saul had
returned from following the Philistines,
that it was told him, saying, "Take note!
David is in the Wilderness of En Gedi."

2 Then Saul took three thousand chosen
men from all Israel, and went to seek David
and his men on the Rocks of the Wild Goats.

3 So he came to the sheepfolds by the road,
where there was a cave; and Saul went in
to attend to his needs. (David and his men
were staying in the recesses of the cave.)

4 Then the men of David said to him, "This
is the day of which the Lord said to you,
'Behold, I will deliver your enemy into
your hand, that you may do to him as it
seems good to you.'" And David arose and
secretly cut off a corner of Saul's robe.

5 Now it happened afterward that David's heart troubled him because he had cut Saul's robe.

6 And he said to his men, "The Lord forbid that I should do this thing to my master, the Lord's anointed, to stretch out my hand against him, seeing he is the anointed of the Lord."

7 So David restrained his servants with these words, and did not allow them to rise against Saul. And Saul got up from the cave and went on his way.

(1 Sam 24:1–7)

7 So David and Abishai came to the people by night; and there Saul lay sleeping within the camp, with his spear stuck in the ground by his head. And Abner and the people lay all around him.

8 Then Abishai said to David, "God has delivered your enemy into your hand this day. Now therefore, please, let me strike him at once with the spear, right to the earth; and I will not have to strike him a second time!"

9 But David said to Abishai, "Do not destroy him; for who can stretch out his hand against the Lord's anointed, and be guiltless?"

10 David said furthermore, "As the Lord lives, the Lord shall strike him, or his day shall come to die, or he shall go out to battle and perish.

11 The Lord forbid that I should stretch out my hand against the Lord's anointed. But please, take now the spear and the jug of water that are by his head, and let us go."

(1 Sam 26:7–11)

For a moment, think about this next question. What would you do if you were not afraid to fail? Most people start dreaming when asked this question. What *would* they do, they ponder. What is your answer?

Here is another question for you. What do you learn when you fail? Many are not prepared to answer this question either. It takes a considerable amount of effort and introspection to discover and to share the answers to those questions. If a fear of failure is holding you back today, my message to you is to shake it off. Let me explain that a little more.

I saw a video recently that featured peacocks. A peacock's body is covered with attractive, colorful feathers. These vibrant, long, blue and green markings on the feathers are a unique feature. The male peacock opens its feathers before it rains and dances to attract female peahens to mate. If the rain is too heavy or too cold, it gradually closes its feathers and shivers. As soon as the rain stops, the peacock shakes itself and all the water falls off of him. He then returns to his full bloom.

What can we learn from that action? Things happen at times to make us pause. To make us have to step back, pivot, or reset the way we are doing something. Like a storm passing over us, if we get rained on, we shiver. But what then? We could seek shelter. We could pause. We could hide. But what then? Do we stop forever? Do we never venture out, even if the sun shines? Do we give up, letting our feathers droop, without any intention of splaying them again? Or should we shake off the droplets once the storm has passed and try again?

John Maxwell wrote in his book *Failing Forward* that sometimes you will win, and sometimes you will learn how to do things differently. He says you should hope to win most of the times and expect to fail some of the times. Regardless of the outcome, you must be ready, willing, and able to live with the results. Do not let the result fold you over until you cannot lift your head and begin again. You are not a failure until you stop trying.

The next time it begins to drizzle, rain, or pour on you, remember, it's your actions during and after the storm that matter.

David Understood Teamwork

Consider today who is surrounding you. In that same book by Maxwell, he said that if you want to go quickly, go alone; and if you want to go far, take a team along with you. It is true, a team is critical for success.

Even an Olympic athlete, while performing on their own, still has a team behind them, helping them to achieve that success.

One is too small of a number to achieve greatness. Jeff Bezos from Amazon is known for his business acumen. Consider the people who work alongside him. Would Amazon be as large of a company as it is today, if there was not almost an entire army of people working there, helping the company to succeed?

Bill Gates is another example. Long after he left Microsoft, it continues to thrive. That is because there are other intelligent people working there. Behind every successful person, you will discover additional and clever people making that achievement possible.

A close examination of this would reveal that many of the high achievers we identify are really captains of very talented teams. The Wright brothers had people who built the airplanes with them. They did not build them alone. Milton Hershey might have created the iconic chocolate bar and foil wrapped kisses we all know, but without workers to build and operate the factory, he would not be a familiar brand.

The best captains are team players. They are not threatened by the gifts and talents of others. They listen, take suggestions and advice, and recognize the gifts of those around them. A true sign of an intelligent leader is the people around them.

"I not only use the brains I have—I use all the brains I can borrow." – Woodrow Wilson

We also have that example in Christ.

12 Now it came to pass in those days that He went out to the mountain to pray, and continued all night in prayer to God.

13 And when it was day, He called His disciples to Himself; and from them He chose twelve whom He also named apostles:

(Luke 6:12–13)

David knew that he must build something bigger than himself.

David Was a Realist, Who Had Faith

The Lord permitted the child that Uriah's wife bore unto David to be stricken with a disease. David fasted and prayed seven days for his son's healing, but the child still died.

15 Then Nathan departed to his house. And the Lord struck the child that Uriah's wife bore to David, and it became ill.

16 David therefore pleaded with God for the child, and David fasted and went in and lay all night on the ground.

(2 Sam 12:15–16)

18 Then on the seventh day it came to pass that the child died. And the servants of David were afraid to tell him that the child was dead. For they said, "Indeed, while the child was alive, we spoke to him, and he would not heed our voice. How can we tell him that the child is dead? He may do some harm!"

19 When David saw that his servants were whispering, David perceived that the child was dead. Therefore David said to his servants, "Is the child dead?"

And they said, "He is dead."

20 So David arose from the ground, washed and anointed himself, and changed his clothes; and he went into the house of the Lord and worshiped. Then he went to his own house; and when he requested, they set food before him, and he ate.

21 Then his servants said to him, "What is this that you have done? You fasted and wept for the child while he was alive, but when the child died, you arose and ate food."

22 And he said, "While the child was alive, I fasted and wept; for I said, 'Who can tell whether the Lord will be gracious to me, that the child may live?'

23 But now he is dead; why should I fast? Can I bring him back again? I shall go to him, but he shall not return to me."

(2 Sam 12:18–23)

David's servants were expecting him to suffer in anguish because of his son's death. They were anticipating he would follow the ritual of mourning, which meant weeping until the third or fourth day, with friends and relatives consoling him. They were astonished that he acted contrary to the custom of mourning over the dead. David confessed his faith in the immortality of the soul and the reality of continued life after death.

In the very next verse, David laid with his wife, Bathsheba, and she had a son, and the Lord loved him.

Then David comforted Bathsheba his wife, and went in to her and lay with her. So she bore a son, and he called his name Solomon. Now the Lord loved him.

(2 Sam 12:24)

Life's Difficulties

To succeed in life, you must learn from losses. Use the reality of that failure to create a growth foundation. You could blame others, rationalize, and make excuses, but it will not change the reality of your situation. Think about a time when you experienced a failure. Did blame, trying to reason, or giving excuses change the situation? Did it make a difference at the moment? There are several realities we learn from David's perseverance. Let's think back to his story. How can that be applied to us, in the present day?

Life Can Be Difficult

One of the problems with modern society is the belief that life is supposed to be simple. That is because we now have so many conveniences. Drive-through restaurants and microwave ovens make meals faster and easier. Cellphone technology allows instant messaging. There is a quick or easy way to do most things. If you don't want to go into the grocery store, you can order online and they bring it to your car. If you don't want to leave the house, with a few clicks your purchase arrives on your doorstep.

Think of all the inventions made to enable you to have that carefree lifestyle. There are products that claim to help you lose weight without exercising, and programs that insist you could make a million dollars from home. The media outlets propagate these advertisements. They understand human behavior and know that people will always look for the quick and easy. Doesn't that sound so much better than hard work and time?

The Bible cautions us not to be gullible.

> *Do not be deceived, God is not mocked; for whatever a man sows, that he will also reap.*
>
> *(Gal 6:7)*

Let no one deceive you with empty words, for because of these things the wrath of God comes upon the sons of disobedience.

(Eph 5:6)

Little children, let no one deceive you. He who practices righteousness is righteous, just as He is righteous.

(1 John 3:7)

Some things are destined to occur in processes and over time. When you plant a seed in the ground, there is nothing you can do to make that seed grow quicker. And when we do intervene to expedite growth, it can be harmful. Imagine a factory where chickens hatch eggs, and six days later they are full grown and ready for consumption. Not all growth is good growth. Even if it's not harmful, it might just not be enjoyable or good.

Have you ever bought produce at the store? It looked beautiful sitting on the display, perhaps red, shining apples. But when you got home, washed one and prepared to take a crisp, juicy bite... there was no flavor. It was void of that which, if it had been allowed the time it needed to ripen naturally, was needed for you to enjoy and be nourished by it.

Every problem is an opportunity and a test of character. Each one produces an occasion for growth. It is up to you if you will let that chance for your personal development to occur. I pray that all of your growth will be ordained by God.

Life is Difficult for Everyone

In the book *Rich Dad, Poor Dad*, the author emphasizes that both the rich and poor have the same twenty-four hours in a day. This is a true fact. I do not have twenty-six, stealing away two hours from your allotment. We each have the same. We all also have struggles, and that means we all have chances to improve, including how we use those precious hours granted to us.

If you are reading this now and secretly wishing that this does not apply to you, I am sorry. No one escapes life's problems, failures, and losses. Large or small, there is always something that happens that you must overcome or rise above.

Even Christ, in the Garden of Gethsemane, had a moment of difficulty.

> *38 Then He said to them, "My soul is*
> *exceedingly sorrowful, even to death.*
> *Stay here and watch with Me."*
>
> *39 He went a little farther and fell on His*
> *face, and prayed, saying, "O My Father,*
> *if it is possible, let this cup pass from Me;*
> *nevertheless, not as I will, but as You will."*
>
> *(Matt 26:38–39)*

Successful people acknowledge their obstacles, confront them, and deal with them. You, too, can move ahead in spite of your circumstances. With your twenty-four hours, you can make the most of them, developing yourself physically, mentally, and spiritually.

Life is More Difficult for Some Than Others

Have you ever been on a cruise ship? Deck chairs on a cruise ship are a big deal. The first challenge is that there may not be enough seats for everyone. Seasoned cruisers know to rise early, claim a chair, and mark it with personal belongings. The second task is to choose one that is facing in the right direction. That begs a question, which way do you prefer to face? Some people place their chairs facing the rear, so they can see where they have been. Others have their chairs forward because they want to see where they are going.

Which of these is you? Do you want to see where you have been or where you are going? What does it matter? Ask yourself the previous question again. Which is more important? To see where you have been or where you are going? To what place should you focus your gaze and your attention?

The Outcome

Three things will happen when you shake it off: (1) recognition comes; (2) rejection ends; and (3) restoration occurs. Let's go a little more in depth with each of these events.

Recognition Comes

Have you studied about the stone which the builder refused? It became the cornerstone with inscriptions written on it. It was a decorative showpiece. Everyone who comes to the building will look at it for inspiration, knowledge, and information.

The stone which the builders rejected
Has become the chief cornerstone.

(Ps 118:22)

When this verse appears in Psalms, it is actually a prophecy of the stoneship of Christ.

Jesus said to them, "Have you never read in the Scriptures: 'The stone which the builders rejected has become the chief cornerstone. This was the Lord's doing, and it is marvelous in our eyes'?

(Matt 21:42)

10 Have you not even read this Scripture: 'The stone which the builders rejected has become the chief cornerstone.

11 This was the Lord's doing, and it is marvelous in our eyes'?"

(Mark 12:10–11)

Then He looked at them and said, "What then is this that is written: 'The stone which the builders rejected has become the chief cornerstone'?"

(Luke 20:17)

This is the 'stone which was rejected by you builders, which has become the chief cornerstone.'

(Acts 4:11)

Coming to Him as to a living stone, rejected indeed by men, but chosen by God and precious,

(1 Pet 2:4)

7 Therefore, to you who believe, He is precious; but to those who are disobedient, "The stone which the builders rejected has become the chief cornerstone,"

8 and "a stone of stumbling and a rock of offense."

(1 Pet 2:7–8)

Think about this rejected stone. It could easily have been part of the structure, bearing load, doing work unrecognized. It could have been one of thousands there, easily passed over by the eye when strolling past. But God wanted Him to be celebrated.

Isaiah 60:19–22. I will rejoice in Schaumburg and take delight in my people. The sounds of weeping and crying shall no more be heard in her.

Isaiah 60:21–2. They will build houses and dwell in them, they will plant vineyards and eat the fruit. No longer will they build houses for others to inhabit, nor plant for others to eat.

19 "The sun shall no longer be your light by day, nor for brightness shall the moon give light to you; but the Lord will be to you an everlasting light, and your God your glory.

20 Your sun shall no longer go down, nor shall your moon withdraw itself; for the Lord will be your everlasting light,

And the days of your mourning shall be ended.

21 Also your people shall all be righteous; they shall inherit the land forever, the branch of My planting, the work of My hands, that I may be glorified.

22 A little one shall become a thousand, and a small one a strong nation. I, the Lord, will hasten it in its time."

(Isa 60:19–22)

As you read these words, I hope they fill you with encouragement. Write these verses down, put them where they can be seen often. On days where you feel lonely, sad, concerned, or anxious, refer back to them.

See the promise here within God's words. Nobody will take your place at work, in your career, family, or business. And your work will receive its due recognition. The everlasting light will erase all mourning.

What of the next step? It's time to explore that one.

Rejection Ends

Rejection is painful. It is activated in the same area of the brain as physical pain. Kirsten Weir wrote an article for the American Psychological Association called "The Pain of Social Rejection".[1] She explained how researchers used a technique to study rejection. They played a game where a subject plays an online game of catch with two other players. Eventually, two of the players deliberately exclude the third person by only throwing the ball to each other. That player began to show "increased activity in the dorsal anterior cingulate and the anterior insula—two of the regions that show increased activity in response to physical pain". The researchers concluded, "As far as your brain is concerned, a broken heart is not so different from a broken arm."

That feeling of exclusion happens to each of us. Sometimes it's done on purpose, other times it's not. It's very likely that we've intentionally or unintentionally caused that feeling to others. When unresolved, that pain created issues in many areas: self-esteem, anger, and chronic self-doubt.

---

1 Weir, Kirsten (2012). "The Pain of Social Rejection". American Psychological Association. Vol 43, No. 4. Retrieved from https://www.apa.org/monitor/2012/04/rejection.

Jer. 8:22 talks about the BALM IN GILEAD to soothe the pain/ loss, restore what you've lost

Ex. 12:31–32 Pharaoh summoned Moses and Aaron by night and told them, get up and go away…… BLESS ME ALSO

Ex. 10:28 Pharaoh had told Moses, "Make sure you never see my face again, for that day you shall die."

Be encouraged in knowing that rejection is temporary. Unless a man under direct orders from God fails Him, it is impossible for him to not accomplish his mission. There is one more part to this equation. Let's examine it closely.

Restoration Occurs

David was fifteen years old when he was anointed by Samuel. You will recall he was thirty years old when he was crowned King of Judah. After that event, he waited another seven years before he became king over all of Israel.

Such patience! It can be hard to wait for something promised. Still, David did not let that waiting cause grumbles or discontent. Throughout the waiting period, he continued to praise God and worship. In fact, David wrote many Psalms during this period, which included Psalm 27.

Ps 27:1–3 The Lord is my light and salvation; Whom shall I fear? The Lord is the strength of my life; Of whom shall I be afraid?

In the first three verses, David gave a tenfold testimony of his confidence in God. He calls Him my light; my salvation, my trust; my strength; my life; my confidence; my protector from the wicked; my protector from enemies; my refuge from the multitudes; and my help in war. There are no complaints. No words of upset or scorn. Even with all of the waiting that he did, not once did David become negative about his circumstances.

Like the magnets you may have played with as a child, give thought to the forces you attract. If you don't like the people who hang around you, you must ask what inside you is attracting them. The change must come from within you. When you see a flower that has bees around it, you can be sure that the flower is sweet. The scriptures talk about this. They say:

A man who has friends must himself be friendly, but there is a friend who sticks closer than a brother.

(Pro 18:24)

This concept reminds me of a song by Michael Jackson, "Man in the Mirror".

Think about who you wish to be and become that person. Look to the scriptures for stories of others who were righteous, caring, and set good examples. Model your behavior after theirs. Then, what you get next is something special. The opportunity.

The Opportunity

God Himself killed Saul, creating the need for a new king.

13 So Saul died for his unfaithfulness which he had committed against the Lord, because he did not keep the word of the Lord, and also because he consulted a medium for guidance.

14 But he did not inquire of the Lord; therefore He killed him, and turned the kingdom over to David the son of Jesse.

(1 Chr 10:13–14)

God will give you opportunities, but you must be prepared to step into them. God will not do for you what you must do for yourself. The men came to David because they saw that he was strong enough to lead them. Life rewarded David for the effort he put forth, but it was God who created the opening.

Opportunity comes to the prepared. David immediately accepted the promotion and was ready to be king. What if he had hesitated? The distance between victory and defeat is short.

What transformation happened? What happened to the others? The Bible does not tell us, but I will share my perspectives from David's point of view and then from the men themselves. The very things that turned David's situation into a lifetime of rejoicing can happen to you.

Use What You Have

David worked with what he had, not what he wanted. The men who came to him looked like they were no good. The opportunities looked useless; the positions appeared to be bleak. There are times when we are also faced with such a challenge. We don't have all of what we think we need in order to have success in achieving the task at hand.

Do you recall, when the Shunammite woman's son died, she saddled up a donkey? A horse would have gotten her there much quicker. However, they did not have horses in the family because they needed donkeys to farm the land.

24 Then she saddled a donkey, and said to her servant, "Drive, and go forward; do not slacken the pace for me unless I tell you."

25 And so she departed, and went to the man of God at Mount Carmel.

(2 Kgs 4:24–25)

Her attitude was that she used what she had to get what she wanted. God will bless you with what you have, not with what you don't have. How does this apply to right now? Your current job might not be ideal right now, but work it. The car in your driveway might not be luxurious, but drive it. A person might not have the desired skill yet when you are needing their help, but be patient with him. Whatever it is, if it appears to be beneath you, manage it well.

Each of these are opportunities for you to trust God. Running into trouble doesn't mean He's not working it out for you. It is a fallacy that if you're doing what God wants you will not run into trouble. Being nice to people does not mean they will be nice back. Paying tithes does not insulate you from financial challenges. Being honest at work does not guarantee you the first promotion. Rain falls on the just and the unjust and sometimes life is not fair.

44 But I say to you, love your enemies,
bless those who curse you, do good to
those who hate you, and pray for those
who spitefully use you and persecute you,

45 that you may be sons of your Father
in heaven; for He makes His sun rise
on the evil and on the good, and sends
rain on the just and on the unjust.

(Matt 5:44–45)

For the vision is yet for an appointed
time; but at the end it will speak, and it
will not lie. Though it tarries, wait for it;

Because it will surely come, it will not tarry.

(Hab 2:3)

Trouble in your life does not mean you will not get the blessing. Delay and difficulty are not synonymous with denial. Do you remember the earlier story of the peacock and the rain? Shake it off, keep praying about that situation, and make your test a testimony.

Mark 10:51. Bartimaeus, what do you want?

Mark 9:23. Do you believe I can help you? I believe help my unbelief.

The Israelites also had trouble. Their temple was destroyed. It needed to be rebuilt, but that led to more difficulties. However, they kept at it, as you will soon read. At the time, they had to shake off their struggles, like the male peacock shakes off the rain, so that their task could be done.

III. Shamgar Against the Odds

Perhaps it feels like in life, the odds are always against you. Everything is out to get you. Is the world so crazy, you just wonder how you will ever get ahead? The story of Shamgar occurs during a low period in Israel. During those times, there was war and disorder. There was so much violence that the people stayed off the road when they traveled.

In the days of Shamgar, son of Anath, in the days of Jael, the highways were deserted, and the travelers walked along the byways.

(Judg 5:6)

To make matters worse, there was no king. The people did what they felt was right. While their decisions were right in their own eyes, that wasn't working out well. Imagine four players around a board game, each with their idea of how the game should be played. This is what was happening then. Everyone made their own rules, and the chaos fueled an invasion by the enemy.

In those days there was no king in Israel; everyone did what was right in his own eyes.

(Judg 21:25)

This verse ends the book of Judges, but it explains why such unlawful acts took place in Israel. There was no legal authority at all. Throughout the entire land, every man made his own laws. These were not true laws, and often conflicted with what another had decreed was a law. Chaos was at a maximum. This was lawlessness in the true sense of the word. Additionally, we know that what the natural man thinks is right is different from following God's law.

The Bible says, "In the days of Shamgar, the highways were deserted and travelers walked along the byways" (Judg 5:6).

Can you imagine that, being so afraid you didn't dare use the main road? Travelers did not go along the road, but they took every form of a shortcut or bypass, and they went through all the bushes. Though it seems almost unimaginable to us that would be safer, the reason is in the very last verse of the book of Judges that I shared. To repeat it: Because in that time, there was no king in Israel and everyone did what was right in their own eyes. That is a formula for disorder, that is an opportunity for those travelers to be preyed upon, hurt, robbed, or even murdered.

Without a king, everyone felt as though they could make their own decisions. If everyone did what seemed right in their eyes, imagine what would happen. If it looks right in your eyes to sit down here, you sit down. If it looks right for you to park here, you park. If it looks right for you to do whatever, you do it. There was complete chaos in the land.

There was war, there was disorder. And so, because of the overlapping and false rules, people did not travel on the highways. They were hiding everywhere that they were going for their safety.

Shamgar's name is only mentioned twice in the Bible, but we can learn a few lessons from him. I want to put his story in the context of today. The Bible says, after the first judge, the ruler, the leader of Israel, there was a man named Shamgar. He was the son of Anath.

Like Samson, Shamgar was strong and powerful, and he killed many men. We do not have a record of how many people Samson killed. We just know it was a lot.

14 When he came to Lehi, the Philistines came shouting against him. Then the Spirit of the Lord came mightily upon him; and the ropes that were on his arms became like flax that is burned with fire, and his bonds broke loose from his hands.

15 He found a fresh jawbone of a donkey, reached out his hand and took it, and killed a thousand men with it.

(Judg 15:14–15)

We know from this scripture that his weapon was the jawbone of a donkey.

Then Samson said: "With the jawbone of a donkey, Heaps upon heaps, With the jawbone of a donkey I have slain a thousand men!"

(Judg 15:16)

But the Bible is telling us that Shamgar alone killed 600 of the Philistines' men with an ox goad. He also did something else incredible. He delivered Israel.

If you can, pause reading this for a moment and search the Internet for a picture of an ox goad. Then imagine the type of warrior it takes to kill 600 men with one and live to talk about it.

Anyone who can win six NBA titles is head and shoulder above his peers. I don't care what else you say about him. Any team that can win championship titles back-to-back-to-back, there's something about them that needs to be looked at. Anybody who can succeed, while everyone around him is failing and falling over, there's something about them that we need to look at. Like the person or like the team, you might not. However, they have a method for success, and it's something that is unique.

The men who Shamgar killed were not together at some point in time because we just heard that the opposition, the Philistines, they never run around together (Judg 3:31) and people did not group themselves together on the highway, so that means that he must have killed them here and there, and not at one single point in time.

Now, if you were not able to find a photo of an ox goad right yet, let me explain it to you. The ox goad is a tool that they used as farmers. One end is sharp, and then the other end has a hook. The hook is used to till the ground. What about the other end? With the point?

Whenever the ox gets tired, the person with him would prod it with that sharp end to encourage the ox to go on along. So, Shamgar using a farm instrument to kill 600 men is unbelievable. That means that this man, in order to be so dexterous, and using an ox goad, must have been a farmer.

He must have been someone who was familiar with that tool and experienced in using it. You know, you cannot know how to use a gun unless you're a gun man. You cannot know how to write code for computers unless you have been trained to do so. You cannot know how to treat people who are sick unless you have gone to medical school. You cannot know what kind of medication the person needs unless you have been to a pharmacy school. In order for Shamgar to know how to use this so well, he must have been a farmer.

Now, how does a farmer out of the middle of nowhere with no background or training become skilled in farming? How does he go from being a nobody to being one of the celebrated leaders in the land so much so that the Bible records his name and they put it there? I want to share several lessons with you about how a person can use something that doesn't look like much of anything to accomplish the will of God in their life. After all, if anything could be said about this man, he was a very unlikely person to become a leader in the land.

Against all the odds that were in his life, he became what God wanted him to become. I want you to think for a minute about what it is in your life that looks impossible. What is it about your life that looks like the odds are stacked against you? Your job? A family issue? Finances? Are you at a crossroads right now, with fire at your back preventing you from turning around?

You have to put these obstacles in the perspective of your life, and look at what it is that God is saying to you.

Shamgar started out as a farmer and gradually worked his way to becoming a judge, a leader, a ruler; one who is above others. What is your limitation today? And how will you get to where you need to go? That's what the secret part is. How to rise above and do what you need to, fulfill your call to God, and man your gates.

Start Where You Are

Many folks are in waiting. They are waiting for the right moment, the right opportunity, the right amount of money, the right recognition, the right street, the right position, the right title.

You are waiting for God to move, but God is waiting for you.

Therefore the Lord will wait, that He may be gracious to you; and therefore He will be exalted, that He may have mercy on you. For the Lord is a God of justice; blessed are all those who wait for Him.

(Isa 30:18)

You all are waiting for God to do this thing, in order for you to do that thing. Here's an example. You are waiting for God to give you a job first, before you will serve Him. You are waiting for God to give you a lot of resources first, before you will find time for Him. You are waiting for God to make everything happen enough for you to testify on His behalf. You are waiting for God, but God is waiting for you.

Therefore the Lord will wait, that He may be gracious to you; and therefore He will be exalted, that He may have mercy on you. For the Lord is a God of justice; blessed are all those who wait for Him.

(Isa 30:18)

This behavior is sending a silent message to God that you will trust Him when you get where you are going, but not until then. It means that God, who you are expecting to do something for you in the future, is not able to satisfy you here and now.

Shamgar started out on a farm. He did not wait until he was accomplished before he began to do what God had him to do. He was fighting on behalf of the land. Let me say this to you today. You need to start from where you are in order to get to where God wants you to go. Let's learn more of this, but through the lens of Nehemiah's Story.

Do you recall in the scriptures how Nebuchadnezzar had destroyed the temple in Jerusalem? The Israelites who had returned were working hard, they were trying to rebuild. There was much happening against them. The work was repeatedly hindered by shortages of the necessary resources, and there was a great deal of external opposition. Eventually, the people become so discouraged that God sent the prophets Haggai and Zechariah to encourage them.

Haggai shared a message with the Israelites. A job half done is not done. He told them, no excuses. Have no distractions. There will always be a distraction. Lastly, he told them no settling, God deserves the best.

Zechariah also had a message: Focus on God's plan, God's purpose. Zechariah motivated the Israelites. Eventually, the temple was completed and dedicated. However, even though these prophets were needed to encourage, motivate, and remind the people what to do, nothing would have happened, had they not started where they were.

Let's talk a little more about their messages.

Do Not Procrastinate

Many of us are waiting for something today.

You will say, "Pastor, I'm coming."

I laughingly say, "Come and do something in the house, or come on and do something in the church."

And they said to me, "Pastor, it's my schedule," or "Pastor, you have to pray with me to come along."

And I say to them, "I can pray with you all you want, but the prayer has to come from inside your heart in that. What is it that you want to do?"

If it feels like I'm talking about you today, don't feel bad because you're not the only one that this is applied to. I've been in that position myself, where it looks like I didn't have time for everything that I wanted to do. But the Bible tells us:

Remember now your Creator in the days
of your youth, Before the difficult days

come, and the years draw near when you say, "I have no pleasure in them":

(Ecc 12:1)

I have a message for our youth today because that is my passion. Do not wait until you have become the partner at your consulting firm. Do not wait until you have your own business before you find time to serve God. I remember, like yesterday, when I was much younger and I served in a church called Freedom Hall. All of us were young people in the church, but we infected each other with enthusiasm; we infected each other with "let's do it". We challenged each other to greater works.

At that time, as I would go to church, the pastor was helping the volunteers who directed people as they parked their cars. They told everyone where to park. They told me where to park and I was like, "What, who is he talking to?"

As the attendants were attempting to direct me to where they wanted me to park, Pastor Tyler came along and he said to me, "Is this where you want to park?"

I said, "Yes."

He told them, "Leave him alone."

That was the last time I parked there, because the next time I came, Pastor Tyler himself was waiting for me. We are of similar ages; he is a couple of years older than me, but because of what he did and who he was, when he said, "Well listen, do you want to park here or will you park where I tell you?"

I said, "Tell me where to park," and I went and I parked where he said.

You see, there's something about what you're doing that you have to learn in order to influence the people around you. It doesn't make a difference what you have or don't have now, but don't procrastinate in what God has told you to do.

When I was talking to someone, and I said to come and do something, he gave one of those answers I often get that are excuses. He said, "Pastor, just pray for me that I will have time."

I replied, "You already have time because both the rich and the poor, they have the same amount of time available to them."

The rich and the poor have this in common,
the Lord is the maker of them all.

(Pro 22:2)

As I shared earlier, we each have the same number of hours in our day. I have the same as you. You have the same as me. Our time allotted each day is equal. However, what you choose to do with your time is in your hands. Let's return to Shamgar. He was told to do something. What happened next? Did he have an excuse that he didn't do it? Was he busy? Tired? Or, did he nod, take up his ox goad, and get to work? Remember the message of Haggai that he shared with the Israelites. A job half done is not done. He told them, no excuses. Have no distractions.

Procrastination is easy to do. But the time for that must pass if you are to man your gates. Vision is one thing that will help you get there.

His Vision

God told Shamgar what he needed to do. Shamgar was a farmer, but God wanted him to serve and to do something for Him. He didn't wait. Shamgar ran and he started. Not only did he run to go and get started, but God gave him a vision for what He wanted Him to do. He saw it.

We have been talking about spiritual warfare for a long time. I have talked before about fighting things and facing invisible things.

If all you see with your eyes is everything that you are seeing, then you have left a lot of things unseen. Let me say that again. If all you see now is what you see, then there are many things in your life you have that you are not seeing.

God told Abraham to lift up his eyes and see all that had been given to him.

14 And the Lord said to Abram, after Lot had separated from him: "Lift your eyes now and look from the place where you are—northward, southward, eastward, and westward;

15 for all the land which you see I give to you and your descendants forever."

(Gen 13:14–15)

Do you think he was talking about the physical things that Abraham was looking at? No. He was talking to him about things that he had not yet seen with his physical eyes. You see, because it is what you see that you will see.

My dad used to tell me, "In the battle of the imagination and the will, your imagination will always win." Let me explain what it was that he meant. Let's imagine that I need to walk on a tightrope between two points. Unless I can see myself walking through it successfully, I will never be able to walk that rope.

This is true of anything. Unless you see yourself operating in that office, accomplishing that goal, or fulfilling that dream, despite how much others encourage you, you will still not see. After the order of Shamgar, I pray God will open your eyes.

My young friends, especially the young ladies, be careful of the type of guy that you are following because many men today are asking their spouses to follow them when they themselves are not going anywhere.

It is very difficult to follow someone who stalled and is not going anywhere. And I say this carefully, because the Bible tells us it is the men who are supposed to see.

A prudent man foresees evil and
hides himself, But the simple
pass on and are punished.

(Pro 22:3)

And it shall come to pass afterward that
I will pour out My Spirit on all flesh; your
sons and your daughters shall prophesy,

your old men shall dream dreams,
your young men shall see visions.

(Joel 2:28)

And it shall come to pass in the last days, says God, that I will pour out of My Spirit on all flesh; your sons and your daughters shall prophesy, your young men shall see visions, your old men shall dream dreams.

(Acts 2:17)

Behold, I will raise them out of the place to which you have sold them, and will return your retaliation upon your own head.

(Joel 3:7)

Recently, I was telling one of my friends in the office how I was watching a basketball game. One of the star players had the ball in his hand. When it was time to pass the ball, he did not look at whether the other player was there, he just took the ball and he passed the ball in that direction. Meanwhile, the player who was supposed to receive the ball had moved out. And because he had moved out, instead of the ball finding its way into the other player's hands, the ball went out of bounds. As I recounted the story, I looked at my friend and said, "That's the position that you need to hold. You see, if you don't hold your position, they'll pass the ball to you and you will not be there. And each of us on the team will lose."

I encourage each of you reading these words to hold your position. We each have a role to play. We each have our designated spot. I need to play my part, you need to play yours, and then, together, God will work with us. That is why the Bible tells us without vision the people perish.

Where there is no revelation,
the people cast off restraint; but
happy is he who keeps the law.

(Pro 29:18)

Where there is no vision, the people perish:
but he that keepeth the law, happy is he.

(Pro 29:18 KJV)

Use What You Have

Let's go back to using what we have been given and what we already have. Shamgar used a simple tool to kill 600 men. Let me ask you. Today, how many problems do you have in your life? Shamgar had 600 problems, and he only had what God gave him.

Listen to me carefully. God will not bless you with what left you. God will not bless you with the person who has walked away from your life. God would not send to you someone who can leave you. If they can walk away, let them go because God will bring someone else into your life.

God will never bless you with someone and say, "Oh, sorry, the person who can bless you is gone, so you are now condemned to a life of misery." When God gets ready to move, you don't need a bunch of stuff. You only need one thing, but God needs to own that.

God Needs to Own It

Shamgar only had an ox goad. He didn't have an armory full of weapons to choose from to attack his enemies. He had his tool that was used to spur oxen. Yet, he didn't complain that he didn't have a sword. He used what he had. Shamgar used his tool to kill 600 Philistines. It was all he had, but God owned it, so it was sufficient. Simon Peter had an ox goad. It was his boat.

1 So it was, as the multitude pressed about Him to hear the word of God, that He stood by the Lake of Gennesaret,

2 and saw two boats standing by the lake; but the fishermen had gone from them and were washing their nets

3 Then He got into one of the boats, which was Simon's, and asked him to put out a little from the land. And He sat down and taught the multitudes from the boat.

(Luke 5:1–3)

This was how Simon Peter made his living. That was how he did everything that he did. Simon Peter did not even go to church, because on the day that Jesus Christ went to him, they were coming from a crusade.

18 And Jesus, walking by the Sea of Galilee,
saw two brothers, Simon called Peter,
and Andrew his brother, casting a net
into the sea; for they were fishermen.

19 Then He said to them, "Follow Me,
and I will make you fishers of men."

(Matt 4:18)

Simon was working. Jesus Christ met him by the side of the road and asked, "Can I use your boat?" (Luke 5:1–3)

You see, the principles always work. It doesn't matter who you are or what circumstances you face, God must own what you have. Trust God to use what you have. By doing so, it will work for a benefit far greater than you can imagine.

I often tell stories from the Bible. Their examples can be brought into modern days, as well. Let me tell you a story about my life. When my wife and I decided that we were going to serve God with whatever it took, we said, "We're going to do this."

So, as we were going on along and serving, I made a decision that whatever it was that we were going to do, I would always build it around serving God.

And whatever you do in word or deed, do all in the name of the Lord Jesus, giving thanks to God the Father through Him.

(Col 3:17)

That is why I'm in church on Sunday mornings, even when I have every reason not to go. There are many days that I travel and go straight from the airport landing with my suitcase in my hand.

I would drag it to church, and people would say, "Pastor, you are late."

I would reply, "I agree, but if it were you, you wouldn't come."

They'd say, "What do you mean?"

I would say, "I'm just coming from the airport. I flew a red eye this morning. I arrived at O'Hare at 5:30 or 6:00. All I did was take a shower and came in here. That's why I'm late. What's your excuse?"

I'm telling you, without any form of contradiction or fear in my heart, the reason why I succeeded to where I am today is because I chose to serve God. That service comes in multiple ways.

Several years ago, there was a person competing against me for a position in Detroit, and I helped him.

He came back and he told me, "Your God must be real good."

I said, "I know."

Like Paul said, I am what I am by the grace of God.

But by the grace of God I am what I am, and His grace toward me was not in vain; but I labored more abundantly than they all, yet not I, but the grace of God which was with me.

(1 Cor 15:10)

I will never fail. I will reach my goal, by the grace of the Lord.

And He said to me, "My grace is sufficient for you, for My strength is made perfect in weakness." Therefore most gladly I will rather boast in my infirmities, that the power of Christ may rest upon me.

(2 Cor 12:9)

It is not you. It is God. If anybody fools you into thinking that you know how to do something, you need to think again, because there are people sharper than you.

I'm sure you all know someone who was better than you academically. You also know someone whose parents were richer than yours, someone who everybody thought would do well in life. I'm not saying that I'm the best person in life now. But when I look at where I am, and all the struggles that I have been through, I can tell Him thank you.

Shamgar's story is a lesson for many of us to learn from. I thought, at some point in time, that I'd be a database administrator and write code for myself. And so, I began to work as an Oracle consultant. Back in the day, they would pay you a lot of money plus cover your travel and expenses. I thought that was my calling.

Twelve of us started. Of the twelve of us that started, only three made any significant progress in that career. Of those three, all three of us today are pastors. Two of them are still in Illinois. I'm not suggesting that you need to be a pastor to succeed where you are, but maybe that was why I succeeded. Or maybe I succeeded because I was a pastor, but when serving God and putting everything with Him, I didn't lack anything.

I would travel back to Chicago on the weekends. There I would stay and study. When I got back on Mondays, whatever the others were studying didn't help them. When the project manager would come, he would bypass me and go and ask them.

One weekend, by the time I got to the office, someone had taken my seat that I used to sit in. They were thinking that when the project manager came, he would come to me this time to ask questions, instead of them. He did not recognize all of us because we looked so alike. He walked past me and went to the end and said, "My friend in the back, I'm sorry that I always ignore you. Let me start from you today." I was already in the front.

When you serve God, He will never let what you're looking for suffer.

I have been young, and now am old; yet
I have not seen the righteous forsaken,
nor his descendants begging bread.

(Ps 37:25)

You see, what is happening is that God will ask you to demonstrate your faith by doing something that is contrary to logic. He's the one who handed it to you. And He's going to ask you to demonstrate your faith in Him by doing something illogical.

David only had a sling and stones, and that is what he used to fight Goliath. And he said, "You come to me with a sword, with a spear, and with a javelin. But I come to you in the name of the LORD of hosts" (1 Sam 17:45) with a stone in his hand and his swinging it against a giant that was much bigger than him. One stone from God will settle the matters of your life.

How Shamgar Become a Judge

I told you that this man rose in rank. He even became a judge. How did he become one, you might wonder.

He became a judge because the Spirit of the Lord came upon him. It was when the Spirit of the Lord came upon him that everything else began to work. When the spirit of God is in your life, you cannot miss it. What you need is to have a relationship with Him.

This is not a relationship that you build with twenty minutes of listening to a sermon on Sunday. You cannot form a relationship with someone in only twenty minutes a week. It takes effort, earnestness, and repetition.

God wants to have a relationship with you.

Now faith is the substance of things hoped for, the evidence of things not seen.

(Heb 11:1)

Jesus said to him, 'You shall love the Lord your God with all your heart, with all your soul, and with all your mind.'

(Matt 22:37)

The Bible says that in time past and in sundry manners, God spoke to us through the prophets, but now He wants to talk to you directly. But God doesn't yell. He tells you in your ear. So, you have to have your own relationship with God. And it is not on Sunday mornings only. That's when we get that relationship. It is on Monday morning, on Tuesday morning, on Wednesday evening, until it gets to a time when God is speaking, and you know it is God talking.

The other day I was driving with my wife and I said, "Someone just came to my mind."

She said, "Call him because when some things come to your mind, you know that there's a lesson inside there."

And so, I called the person, and he said, "Oh, I was just thinking about you."

My wife looked at me and said, "Didn't I tell you?"

When you have a relationship, you will know what the other will want before they finish. My wife can finish my sentences. That is the way that it needs to be. I pray that you will find your own spare parts.

Remember, if God wants to bless you, He will do it in such a way that it will spill over to everyone who's around you. Isn't that such a wonderful thing to have and to be given? Do you recall this story?

5 But Simon answered and said to Him, "Master, we have toiled all night and caught nothing; nevertheless at Your word I will let down the net."

6 And when they had done this, they caught a great number of fish, and their net was breaking.

7 So they signaled to their partners in the other boat to come and help them. And they came and filled both the boats, so that they began to sink.

(*Luke* 5:5–7)

They were blessed. God's gift spilled over them. So, now you have your ox goad in your hands, and you're saying, "This was meant for me, for my business, for my career, and it is not enough. I want to keep it to myself."

But look at what God did with Shamgar. Because Shamgar had a relationship with God, he knew where to start, what to use, and what to do to glorify God. You want God to help you, and he is waiting for you.

There might be a crisis in your life causing you to think it's helpless. Even strong men have times where they experience weakness or sorrow. Nehemiah was faced with such a thing. He was told the wall of Jerusalem was broken down. The gates had been burned with fire. What did he do? He heard what happened. He sat, then wept. Nehemiah mourned for a time, he fasted, and then he prayed to God. He had a relationship with God, and that helped him to move forward in this difficult time.

It was time then he inspected the damage. Nehemiah went to Jerusalem. The walls were broken, but the gates were burned. This was both a physical and a spiritual event. Physically, there were broken walls and burned gates. Spiritually, there were a variety of teachings that could be learned from this.

IV. What is Your Story?

The best thing that God has ever done for man is salvation. Everything else comes on the platform of salvation. There is a song with the lyrics, "He saved me, and He washed me with blood. And for the fact that I have been saved and I've been joined here with Christ, every other thing."

That is why Jesus said, "Seek ye first the Kingdom of God and His righteousness and all other things shall be added unto you" (Matt 6:33). Thank God that you are saved. Everything is permitted to happen in your life because you are saved. Because of your new birth, you can enjoy His blessings. You can enjoy His love. It is by His gift of salvation that you can enjoy everything that you are enjoying today.

And Joses, who was also named
Barnabas by the apostles (which is
translated Son of Encouragement),
a Levite of the country of Cyprus,

(Acts 4:36)

I want you to take note of a few things in this passage. The man's name was Joses, but he was named Barnabas. He was not named by his parents. The Bible says, "But by the apostles." Who were the apostles? Those were the leaders in the church. They were this man's contemporaries, the people who were around him and who knew him well. They named him Barnabas. Barnabas in the original Greek was translated to mean "the son of encouragement".

Every fact is scripture and is relevant. Look at the next point in this passage. It says he was a Levite. Levites were not known for their wealth. They were not known for their largeness. They were known as being disciples. They were known as being ministers. They were known as being consecrated, and honored, and focused on serving God. So, he was a Levite and he was from the country of Cyprus. Cyprus was not where the Christians came from. He was an aberration. He was an oddity. He was not one of those that you will expect to be called the Son of Encouragement.

Having land, sold it, and brought the
money and laid it at the apostles' feet.

(Acts 4:37)

There's another interesting fact. He had land. That was unusual for a Levite. It had probably been handed down to him as a family inheritance. And what did he do with the land? He sold it. And after he sold it, he brought the money and laid it at the feet of the apostles.

Let me pause the story for a moment. We all had nicknames when we were growing up. Every one of us. Whether it was something they called you in school, a title you earned, or someone looked at you and for whatever reason decided they were going to call you by that name, you had one. And many of those names we are not happy to carry. We did not all get a nickname like Son of Encouragement.

I have a brother. When he was younger, we used to call him a name. Now that he is married, every time we call him the name, his wife will say, "Listen, I don't want you to call my husband that name again."

I reply, "But you don't know what it means."

She says, "I've learned what it means. I just don't want you to call him that name again."

There are many of us that had names like that, but look at what the Bible says concerning this man. It says he was the Son of Encouragement. What a testimony. What a story.

Now, I said that he was not a likely person to have that nickname. At this time in his story, the church had just scattered. Saul had just finished bringing down fire upon them. Jesus Christ was dead. They had just gotten power from on High. Nobody knew them at this point in time. They were running in chaos.

We've been talking about emotional well-being and mental wellness a lot lately. In the middle of all the things that you are going through, can someone look at you and want to be like you? Can someone look at you and say, "You are the son or daughter of encouragement?"

It is important for you to know what people say about you. What is it that people say concerning you? What is your testimony? Would they say you are a grumpy person or a happy person? Would they say you are an unkind or a generous person? Would they leave if they saw you coming or prefer to be around you? It is critical that you know.

Even Jesus Christ wanted to know what people said about Him.

*27 So the men marveled, saying,
"Who can this be, that even the
winds and the sea obey Him?"*

*28 When He had come to the other side,
to the country of the Gergesenes, there
met Him two demon-possessed men,
coming out of the tombs, exceedingly
fierce, so that no one could pass that way.*

*29 And suddenly they cried out, saying,
"What have we to do with You, Jesus,
You Son of God? Have You come here
to torment us before the time?"*

(Matt 8:27–29)

*13 When Jesus came into the region
of Caesarea Philippi, He asked His
disciples, saying, "Who do men say
that I, the Son of Man, am?"*

*14 So they said, "Some say John
the Baptist, some Elijah, and others
Jeremiah or one of the prophets."*

*15 He said to them, "But who
do you say that I am?"*

*16 Simon Peter answered and said, "You
are the Christ, the Son of the living God."*

(Matt 16:13–16)

What do people say about you? What is your story? You see, you must be an encourager of destiny and encourage all people around you, regardless of what you yourself are going through. Is that difficult?

Nicholas James Vujicic is an Australian American Christian evangelist and motivational speaker. He was born with tetra-amelia syndrome, which is a rare disorder characterized by the absence of arms and legs. At the beginning of his life, he felt sorry for himself. Now he is thirty-eight years old, married with four children, and traveling the world, encouraging people and leading them to Christ. People pay thousands of dollars to go and listen to this man speak, and all because he decided that he wants to be an encourager. Can you encourage someone where you are today despite your circumstances?

Let's return to the Bible. Barnabas sold his land and brought the money to church. This teaches us several lessons.

First, he understood generosity. He did not have to sell the land. And if he sold it, he could have used the money for something else, but he had the proper perspective on money. I tell people that money is neither good nor bad. It doesn't change you. It just makes you more of who you are. You may see someone and others say, "Oh, he has so much money now he has forgotten God." It's not because of the money this person forgot God. He never remembered Him in the first place.

One of the wealthiest artists today is famous for the Madea Family series. I'm sure you know who I'm talking about. It is said when the man was going to build the foundation of his studio, he buried thousands of Bibles inside there. I'm not saying that you should go and do that as a talisman, but the fact that you can even imagine that you want Bibles to be the foundation of what you are doing speaks volumes about who you are and what you believe in. He didn't have to do it, because the Bible does not have anything to do with the strength of the building. He was not going to the physical strength of the building; he was going to the spiritual strength of the building. He understood what it is.

But what is it about generosity that's so important? The Bible tells us that the generous soul will prosper. The generous soul will be made rich. The generous soul will have largesse, because he who waters will himself also be watered. It is the watering hose principle. You have a watering hose. You connect it to a pipe. As long as the water continues to flow through the hose, the hose will never be dry. Barnabas understood the principles of generosity.

Second, he was committed to his cause. He was committed to his commitment. When he said, "I'm coming," he showed up. When he said, "I will call you," he called. When he said, "I'll be there," he was there. And not only that, but he also took all that he had. Remember, he was a Levite, so he had much and he put it down as his cause. How strange that might have seemed to some.

I remember when my elder sister decided that she wanted to give her life to Christ. It worked for her, but it didn't work for me. She had been a woman who wore a lot of make-up and fancy clothing. One day she came home and said, "I have chosen to become a Christian."

And she went from being this fancy, high-flying woman, to being this dowdy-looking, dull-dressing example of nothing. I said to her one day, "Sis, if this is what Christianity is, if it takes you from being a good-looking woman to this, I don't think I want to be a Christian. This is not the testimony that I want."

She responded to me, "You don't understand." She said, "As long as I can look at myself and not see change, nothing inside me will change."

So, what worked for her was that she had to take away all the clothes that she was wearing before and discard them, so that when anybody now saw her, they would ask, "What happened?"

Then, she would reply, "I've changed my lifestyle."

And she explained to me, "To everyone looking at me who would know that my lifestyle has changed, they will expect to hold me to that new lifestyle, and that's why I have chosen to look the way that I look now."

It took me a long time to understand it, but now I get it. You must be committed to your commitments.

Next, Barnabas understood spiritual authority.

John answered and said, "A man can receive nothing unless it has been given to him from heaven."

(John 3:27)

A man can receive nothing unless it is given to him from above, from heaven. The Spirit governs time and chance.

Finally, he understood what it meant to become a great influence.

1 But a certain man named Ananias, with
Sapphira his wife, sold a possession.

2 And he kept back part of the proceeds, his
wife also being aware of it, and brought a
certain part and laid it at the apostles' feet.

(Acts 5:1–2)

Ananias and Sapphira wanted to be like Barnabas. They sold their own land, but instead of bringing the money, they did something else with it. They wanted to be like him, and they had things that they wanted, but they were not willing to pay the same price.

Imitate me, just as I also imitate Christ.

(1 Cor 11:1)

And the things that you have heard
from me among many witnesses,
commit these to faithful men who
will be able to teach others also.

(2 Tim 2:2)

That's why Paul said, "Imitate me as I imitate Christ." Who are you imitating? Who is imitating you? A mentor is someone who teaches people coming after him. It must be deliberate. As a mentor, you must be committed to teaching somebody something. And you are never too young to be a mentor. The same thing goes with being a mentee. You are never too old to learn. So, the question for you today is, "Are you a good influence?"

And when Saul had come to Jerusalem,
he tried to join the disciples; but they
were all afraid of him, and did not
believe that he was a disciple.

(Acts 9:26)

Why were the disciples afraid when Saul came to Jerusalem and tried to join them? They did not believe he was a disciple because prior to this time he was the one who was killing disciples. He took special permission to go and kill them. He then showed up and wanted to be a disciple. Of course, they felt that perhaps he was trying to deceive them. To them, it was a logical thought. Why is this story important? What made this man who would kill another suddenly want to become a disciple?

But Barnabas took him and brought
him to the apostles. And he declared
to them how he had seen the Lord on
the road, and that He had spoken to
him, and how he had preached boldly
at Damascus in the name of Jesus.

(Acts 9:27)

It says, "But Barnabas..." Every time you see "but", it is a change of tone to negativity. They didn't believe him. They thought it was not possible. They thought he was just looking for a way to infiltrate so that he could gather all of them to kill them. It says, "But Barnabas took him and brought him to the apostles, and he declared to them how he had seen". This man had changed. His word was good. His reputation was enough to benefit the people who were around him. The thing that they said was not possible, he showed was possible.

When you hear that word, "impossible", it is not a fact. It is an opinion of the person who is saying it. Let me repeat that so you can quote me. The word impossible is not a fact. It is the opinion of the person who is saying it. They said Saul was a killer. He could never become a disciple. And so, they ran away from him. You see, anything is impossible until somebody does it. Once somebody does it, the impossible now becomes possible. But yet, you may say science has proven that some things are impossible. Go back and look at that thing again. There is so much that science told us last week, last month, or last year was not possible, that now this same science has changed the story to tell it is possible. Things that are impossible remain so until someone does them.

Have you ever heard of Roger Bannister? He was the first person to run a mile in under four minutes. Until he did it, everyone said that it was not possible to run a mile so quickly. Since then, thousands of people have done it simply because they have seen it done and know it is possible. That is just one example of what was impossible once before today is now possible.

And let me add this thought for you to ponder as well. The 80/20 rule always operates. If you are not familiar with that rule, it says that 80% of the work is always done by 20% of the people. On the flip side, 20% of the work accomplishes 80% of the things that need to happen. I put it that this is true about anything in life. Whatever looks impossible today is 80% in your mind and 20% in your body. If you can believe that it will work, you can make it happen because the battle has to be won in your mind. Everybody in life needs a strategy for something that you want to do.

For example, today, many Americans are overweight. The stories you will hear people tell is, "I've tried everything". Have they really tried everything? I used to tell myself my weight problem was because I had big bones. That was my excuse for being overweight. There are so many excuses out there, not just for weight problems, but for everything. Procrastination, vulgar language, the way we treat others. Why, everything we do could have an excuse if we looked for one.

I want to tell you that you can change your story so that people will know you for something different. Something better. Something great. Something incredible. You have to divorce yourself from the story of your limitations. Marry yourself to the truth of your unlimited capacity. If you do, God will make all things possible for you.

You have to change your story. And to change your story, it's all in your hands. Every bit of this is up to you, and you are the only one who can make it work. However, you are not alone in creating this change. The almighty God will give you the strength. He will give you the wisdom, the understanding, and the faith to go ahead and change your story, even in these circumstances of time.

V. Breakthrough

Have you ever observed a gate? Gates have two functions. They keep people or things out and they keep people or things in. A gate is also the center of power and authority. You need to be in charge of your gates. Eye gate, mouth gate, ear gate; nothing happens until you are changed from inside out. Do you remember some of the most famous gates in the Bible? Let's talk a little about Jericho.

Now Jericho was securely shut up because of the children of Israel; none went out, and none came in.

(Josh 6:1)

And the Lord said to Joshua: "See! I have given Jericho into your hand, its king, and the mighty men of valor."

(Josh 6:2)

24 And it happened after this that Ben-Hadad king of Syria gathered all his army, and went up and besieged Samaria.

25 And there was a great famine in Samaria; and indeed they besieged it until a donkey's head was sold for eighty shekels of silver, and one-fourth of a kab of dove droppings for five shekels of silver.

(2 Kgs 6:24–25)

In these verses, we see the city has been shut in because of the children of Israel. To besiege means to lay ambush, as in they are waiting for them. Indeed, it was besieged until the donkey's head was sold for eighty shekels of silver. That was approximately the average wage for two and a half years. Imagine spending two and a half years of wages to buy the head of a donkey.

One-fourth of a cup of dove was also expensive. A dove is a small bird. The cup of the dove is the waste or the excrement. I'm not trying to gross you out. I'm just painting a picture. A quarter of that was being sold for approximately two and a half months of wages. Why? That dove's waste cannot do anything. It doesn't satisfy, so it doesn't make sense to use money you don't have to buy something that cannot bring any satisfaction. This was the condition that was in the land at that time.

Then, as the king of Israel was passing by on the wall, a woman cried out to him, saying, "Help, my lord, O king!"

(2 Kgs 6:26)

For a moment, let's talk about the wall. There was a wall that surrounded the city, and that was why they could not go in. To explain briefly about the cities back then, ancient cities were built with walls around them.

These walls were very wide and they had gates. They were so wide that people lived on top of the walls.

Then she let them down by a rope
through the window, for her house was
on the city wall; she dwelt on the wall.

(Josh 2:15)

Rahab is who the scriptures are talking about. She lived on top of the wall. The gates we read about in Joshua 6:1 were a feature of all of the city walls. Nothing came in or went out that did not go through the walls. The walls were meant for protection. The people living there thought the walls protected them, but they did not know that protection only comes from God. There was a way around that wall that did not go through the wall or through the gates.

Consider, for a moment, that you are a city. Where are your walls? What are your walls? There is a wall of wisdom, a wall of understanding, a wall of strategy, that I pray God will give to every one of us today in the name of Jesus Christ.

6 And the king and his men went to
Jerusalem against the Jebusites, the
inhabitants of the land, who spoke to
David, saying, "You shall not come in here;
but the blind and the lame will repel you,"
thinking, "David cannot come in here."

7 Nevertheless David took the stronghold
of Zion (that is, the City of David).

8 Now David said on that day, "Whoever climbs up by way of the water shaft and defeats the Jebusites (the lame and the blind, who are hated by David's soul), he shall be chief and captain." Therefore they say, "The blind and the lame shall not come into the house."

(2 Sam 5:6–8)

The first assignment that David had when he became king was to go and overtake and overcome Jerusalem. Some told him, "You are just a clown, no king before you has done it and you will not be an exception." However, in verse seven, the Bible says, "David took the stronghold." He took it. And after he had taken the stronghold, he renamed the city of Jerusalem to the City of David. I pray that whatever the problem you have, the almighty God will give you the ability to rename that problem by yourself, just like David did when he conquered that which others thought he could not do.

It doesn't matter what others say. Be courageous and set forth. If you have been called sick, I pray that you will become known as one who was healed. If you have been known as the one who was unemployed, may people know you by the demerits of your life. That man who didn't have work, that man who was not married, that man who was sick, or whatever, I pray God will change that name for you today in the name of Jesus Christ.

Let's go now and explore how David took the city that no one else had been able to capture. It's an amazing story.

In verse eight, David said on that day, "Whoever climbs up by the way of the water shaft". The way of the water shaft was the way that they went.

The walls were there. The gates were there. It appeared as though they could not get through, but there was a way under it, which was the water shaft. And if you went in through the water shaft, you could go in and out and win without fighting. Can you imagine such a thing? They won without fighting that day.

One of the main purposes of those city gates was everything went through there. Anyone who wanted to sell in the city went through the gates. Anyone who wanted to live in the city went through the gates. It was a center of commerce, and important transactions were announced there. It was almost like the stock exchange today, when they have the opening bell of the stock market ringing in the morning. This was what was going on there. The city gates were the court or the legal system. If you had something you needed to decide, people convened there and they went to meet the elders of the community, waiting for them at the city gates. Deuteronomy 21:18–19 even shows us parents of rebellious children would be at the gates. The adults brought the children before the elders and said, "Help us deal with them."

The gates also served the purpose of being the news dissemination center. If you wanted to send something or tell everybody something, it was there that public announcements were heralded. The city and the walls were important. In fact, for some, the walls even decided their future.

Then it happened, when he made mention of the ark of God, that Eli fell off the seat backward by the side of the gate; and his neck was broken and he died, for the man was old and heavy. And he had judged Israel forty years.

(1 Sam 4:18)

When Israel was fighting the Philistines, Eli mentioned the ark of God and fell off the gates! That was where he was when they took the news of what was going on to him.

David also made use of the gates. That's where he was going to announce he was fighting his son Absalom. Remember, the gates of the city were not just a center of commerce or a place granting entry to the city. It was placed where information was shared and the center of power and authority. That is why Genesis 22:17 says, "Your children will take possession of the gates of their enemies." It didn't say they would possess their lives. It said, "the gate" because if you possess the gate, that means you will possess power over them. You possess influence over them. You possess their ears and you possess their hearts.

These gates are a metaphor for your life and mine. This is what Jesus was talking about in Matthew 16:18, "And I also say to you that you are Peter, and on this rock I will build My church, and the gates of Hades shall not prevail against it."

He was not talking about the gate of the physical church. He was talking about the gate of the church that was dispersed. Now, if He's talking about you manning the gates of your life, you want to understand what those gates are. You need to be in charge of your gates. Let's talk a little about a few of those gates.

Eye Gate

The first gate I will tell you about is the eye gate.

The lamp of the body is the eye. If therefore your eye is good, your whole body will be full of light.

(Matt 6:22)

The scripture says that the eye is the lamp of the body. If your eyes are healthy, then your whole body will be full of light. What does an eye have to do with a body made full of light? Isn't the eye just to see? The Bible has something to say about that.

But if your eye is bad, your whole body will be full of darkness. If therefore the light that is in you is darkness, how great is that darkness!

(Matt 6:23)

Your eyes say a lot about the gates. They are access into your being, the same way when Jesus Christ was saying that "Your children will possess the gates of the enemy and the gates of hell will not prevail against your life."

They're talking about the gates that are completely around you. You need to manage and to take charge of the gates into your soul and your being. The eye gate is one of the most important.

And the Lord said to Abram, after Lot had separated from him: "Lift your eyes now and look from the place where you are—northward, southward, eastward, and westward;"

(Gen 13:14)

The eyes signify many things, and it's important they be enlightened.

The eyes of your understanding being enlightened; that you may know what is the hope of His calling, what are the riches of the glory of His inheritance in the saints,

(Eph 1:18)

But what of the other gates? Is there another we need to be mindful of?

Mouth Gate

The second gate we examine is the mouth gate.

17 Do you not yet understand that whatever enters the mouth goes into the stomach and is eliminated?

18 But those things which proceed out of the mouth come from the heart, and they defile a man.

(Matt 15:17–18)

It is not what goes into your mouth, but what comes out of your mouth that creates a problem in life; not what you eat, but what you say. Everything in life was created by mouth. When God was going to make the Earth in Genesis Chapter 1, the Bible tells us God said, "*Let there be a firmament in the midst of the waters, and let it divide the waters from the waters.*" *(Gen 1:6)*. Everything was created by what was said, all of creation. In Mark 11:24, Jesus told us, "Therefore I say to you, whatever things you ask when you pray, believe that you receive *them*, and you will have *them*."

How powerful words are! Anything that you ask in prayer and believe in, is what you get. That's the mouth gate. But what of another?

Ear Gate

The third gate is the ear gate, meaning that which you hear.

If anyone has ears to hear, let him hear.

(Mark 4:23)

This verse talks about what you hear. It says that if any man has ears, "Let him hear."

That means that there are some people who have ears and yet they don't listen. I'm sure you all know someone who has ears, or at least it looks like it, but they can't hear or they hear, but they don't listen, or they listen and you can't tell. It's a problem. God is constantly speaking to people who have ears. Are you listening? Are you hearing what He is telling you? I'm praying that God will open your ears to His Word.

Learning to hear God's voice is a little like training a pet. When we were younger, my dad had all sorts of animals. We had rabbits, geese, cats, parrots, and dogs. Our house was like a zoo. Back then we didn't name our dogs. Our dog was just named Doggy. And when anybody would come to the gate, the only thing that the dog would do is run out of the house. You would think it was coming to stop you. But if you opened the gate, the dog would go out before you could come in. The only person that dog respected was my dad. If my dad opened the gate, the dog would immediately stand and wag his tail. For anybody else, he would ignore them. He recognized the voice of my father. It is critical that you and I recognize the voice of God, our Father, when He's talking to us.

In Luke 1:31, the angel said to Mary, "And behold, you will conceive in your womb and bring forth a Son, and shall call His name Jesus." Immediately Mary heard that, and became pregnant by what she heard. Many people lose their salvation by what they hear. I don't know what you are listening to, but you need to change the channel to which your ears are tuned so you can go ahead and listen to something that brings life and not death. Why is it important that we're talking about taking charge of your gates? It is because everything that is in your environment comes into you and settles down in your pit, in your heart, in your stomach.

All those gates feed your heart. And that is why in Proverbs 4:23, the scripture tells us, "Keep your heart with all diligence, for out of it *spring* the issues of life." But how do you guard your heart? It is by guarding what goes into your heart, by taking charge of what enters into your spirit. It is by taking charge of what enters into the things that you are hearing. If all you are hearing about is death, very soon you will be dreaming about dying.

If all you hear are words of affirmation or words of encouragement, you will get up and feel like you are a lion of the tribe of Judah. And you will want to do things that only the son of the lion can do. You know the son of a lion is a lion. A lion does not give birth to a dog. It's not possible. The lion does not let anyone else tell him he is something he is not. What are you listening to? What you hear and see and say guards and brings about your heart. It brings about the breakthrough and the changes that you need in life.

Imagine you have an upcoming exam or job interview. What if someone says, "You can't pass that exam," or "You won't get that job". If you can't see yourself being victorious, then what chance do you have? "I can pass that exam" or "I can get that job" is what you should say.

This is why today you have to guard what is on the inside of you. Don't listen to what others are saying. What somebody says about you does not have to become your reality. What people around you think about you is their business. What are you listening to today?

For with the heart one believes unto righteousness, and with the mouth confession is made unto salvation.

(Rom 10:10)

This goes two ways. When you see someone and you hear what they're saying from their mouth, you will know what is going on in their hearts. The same is also true for you. Here's another example. If you knock over a glass of orange juice, water will not pour out. If you open a bottle of Coke, mango juice will not come out of it. It is whatever is in the heart that spills out of the mouth. That's why the Bible says, "Hear, my son, and be wise; and guide your heart in the way" (Pro 23:19b) because what you say is what you are going to get. Nothing happens until you are changed from the inside out. If you give money to an uneducated man, once he finishes spending it he will become broke again. Think of those who have won millions in the lottery, but they quickly become broke again because they never understood from the inside that you plant seeds.

Up, Zion! Escape, you who dwell with the daughter of Babylon.

(Zech 2:7)

It is possible for you to deliver yourself from where you are. Many people don't know it or don't understand it, but you can deliver yourself from the hand of whatever it is that is oppressing you. I don't know what is oppressing you today or what it is that you're struggling with. But you can deliver yourself from the things that are challenging your life today.

That refers to anything that is anti-God, fighting against the will of God for your life, or laying siege upon you. Anything that obstructs your joy or forcibly controls or imprisons certain parts of your life requires a breakthrough.

Take charge of the thing that will keep parents from enjoying their life. Take charge of the thing that holds children bound in some form of affliction.

I don't know what it is that you are dealing with, but in Job 22:28, the Bible says that "You will also declare a thing, and it will be established for you;" Who is going to declare? I, myself, can declare. And I will. But it says in Job 22:28, "You will also declare a thing, and it will be established for you" so light will shine on your ways.

What were we talking about when the eyes are good? "Light will come." So, when you decree a thing, the light comes, your eyes see and your way is right. Do you get the interrelationship? That is why today you must take charge of your gates. Whatever things come into your heart and your spirit; you are allowing it. You can't pass that exam, says who? You can get promoted.

If you try and stand in the way, God will bulldoze you. You will not get approved. You cannot tell me I won't pass an exam. You can tell me you won't do it for me, but you can't tell me I won't pass. That is beyond your pay grade. My life is not in your hands. You cannot tell me that I will not have children. Who are you? In this land, God has decided that none shall be barren and if it is you who will keep me from having children, God will have to remove you.

Whatever it is, whoever it is that is standing in the way of your progress in life, God almighty will answer them by Himself. Your response should be a declaration. What you declare shall be established for you.

What you want to do is to ask God this, "Make me an excellent ornament in your house." The Bible tells us that there are ornaments of silver and gold and wood, and God only likes the best. "My Father, make me an excellent ornament that is worthy to decorate Your presence."

Ezra was such an ornament. After a while, Ezra took priests, singers, ushers, and servants and went back for the Israelites who were still captive. He led them to Jerusalem and taught them the word of God. That's not all he did. He also restored worship and imitated reforms. Gatekeepers were trained, and singers sang continual praise. There were more guards now, as those who lived there were appointed. Some were in their homes as guards, others at specific posts. With all of his absolute care in hearing and seeing the problem and working toward making change, Ezra causes a spiritual revival.

VI. Beyond Your Eyes

To take charge of your gates, it is time to return to the eyes. Let's start with the first few verses of Genesis 13:

1 Then Abram went up from Egypt,
he and his wife and all that he had,
and Lot with him, to the South.

2 Abram was very rich in livestock,
in silver, and in gold.

3 And he went on his journey from
the South as far as Bethel, to the
place where his tent had been at the
beginning, between Bethel and Ai,

4 to the place of the altar which he had
made there at first. And there Abram
called on the name of the Lord.

5 Lot also, who went with Abram,
had flocks and herds and tents.

(Gen 13:1–5)

To break this down, verse by verse, let's look at this closely.

1. Abram was a rich man.
2. He continued to be a wanderer, even though he was affluent. If you don't know what you seek, how do you know when you've found it?

3. He went back to the starting point. Abram wandered until he came back to the place where he originally was. It is true that the grass often appears greener on the other side.
4. He returned to the site where he had built an altar, and then he prayed there. All roads lead back to God.
5. Lot also became rich, by benefit of association.

Wisdom, Knowledge, and Understanding

These are three words that are often used together.

Wisdom is the principal thing;
therefore get wisdom. And in all
your getting, get understanding.

(Pro 4:7)

This concept is what made Solomon stand out among kings. He understood the differences: *knowledge* is information; *understanding* is comprehension; and *wisdom* is application.

You can know something and not understand. You can understand, but not apply. Nothing is complete until it is applied. Wisdom is the application of knowledge.

Consider, for example, a physician who smokes cigarettes. He has knowledge without wisdom. You can have knowledge and still hurt yourself by doing the wrong thing.

Do you attend church regularly? What do you do with the information you receive? If you are receiving information every week to facilitate life-changing transformation, it should be made manifest in your prayer life, faith level, and commitment to Christ.

But to those who are called, both
Jews and Greeks, Christ the power
of God and the wisdom of God.

(1 Cor 1:24)

Jesus is called the wisdom of God. He is God applied. Make sure that while you are reading this book, you get the teaching and apply it until it becomes wisdom to you.

Vision-Eyes Have the Nature of Destroying Barriers

Your life is the result of what you see, your vision for yourself, and what you can see yourself doing. Vision demands the destruction of barriers. It is the capacity to see beyond barriers.

In the most recent presidential election, history was made again. Following the election and re-election of America's first African American president (2008; 2012), Joe Biden became president on his third run (1988; 2008; 2020), the oldest candidate yet. Kamala Harris is the 49th and current vice president of the United States. She is the first female vice president and the highest-ranking female official in U.S. history, as well as the first African American and first Asian American vice president.

Many may have thought none of these individuals could achieve what they did. Perhaps, it was even labeled impossible. Impossible is the opinion of the speaker. What can you see yourself doing? Do you see yourself doing something others think might be impossible? In some homes, parents have eyesight, and they plot a path for their children. For many, the vision is their own. Vision is what makes a man travel to new shores in hope of a better future. It is what makes a person return to school. It makes people start up a business when they are seventy years old.

We can learn a lot about vision from eagles. Let's consider how their vision distinguishes them. Vision is what makes the eagle the king of birds. They can see clearly, in detail, for up to two miles. An eagle can also spot a rabbit two and a half miles away. It can see fish below the surface of water. That could be considered impossible to some, but the eagle has no doubt in its mind it can do these things.

Vision is the key to your life having meaning. Let's stay with the eagle analogy a bit longer.

Eagles fly higher than any other bird. They have the ability to set their wing bones into a locked position and ride the winds. These large birds also soar into storms. The bigger the storm, the higher they soar. They use their problems to go higher and higher. Falling is not an option.

Eagles never flock, and do not have or keep a lot of company. Pigeons do. Which bird would you be? The one that is strong and acts individually like an eagle, or the one that hides in the crowd like a pigeon?

In flight, Eagles do not meet other birds unless they are also eagles. If you keep running into pigeons, you need to change the altitude where you fly. You can tell where you are in life by the people you keep meeting. Are they complaining or dissatisfied? Are they soaring?

Choose Your Friends Based on Destination

Can two walk together,
unless they are agreed?

(Amos 3:3)

He who walks with wise men
will be wise, but the companion
of fools will be destroyed.

(Pro 13:20)

If you are walking with people who are not in agreement with God's will for your life, you may need to change your associations. He who walks with the wise, will be wise, and the companion of fools will be destroyed.

Lot became successful by hanging out with Abram (Gen 13:5–6). David's vagabonds became his mighty men (1 Chr 12:1–2; 16–22). Choose your associations by your destination. God will allow you to meet people who will take you to another level. You need associates who will encourage you, challenge you, and keep you flying.

Let's go back to the birds again. Consider how geese fly in formation. Scientists have determined that the V-shaped formation geese use when migrating serves two important purposes: it conserves their energy, and each bird flies slightly higher than the bird in front of them, resulting in a reduction of wind resistance.

These birds work together. They help each other. By doing so, they are all successful in reaching the destination that they were trying to get to. By surrounding yourself with those who will help you, and who can succeed with your help, you will all be able to reduce resistance and reach your goals. Now, let's dig a little into the differences between sight and vision.

Sight Versus Vision

The greatest gift God gave to man is vision, which includes sight. Sight is a function of the eyes; vision is a function of the heart. God never intended for us to live by our eyes. The just shall live by their faith (Rom 1:17, Gal 3:11, Heb 10:38). The content of the heart is what matters most.

Vision is limited by the boundary of your imagination. Eyes are limited to what you can see. That is why the scriptures teach us to walk by faith and not by sight (2 Cor. 5:7). If we could learn to live with our eyes closed, our hearts could take over our lives.

Eyes Show You What Is—Vision Shows You What Could Be

Faith is the substance of things hoped for, evidence of things your eyes cannot see (Heb 11:1). Vision releases you to the uncharted frontiers of the future.

There is value in history. It is good to understand and celebrate what you have accomplished. The caution is to not become so attached to the 'good ole days' that you do not create new ones. God wants us to live by the vision in our heart, and not the sight in our eyes.

Vision being the capacity to see further than your eyes can look is the greatest source of hope. It is encouragement for every time you have seen yourself doing things, but were disappointed in your efforts. Do not be discouraged, it simply may be that it has not come to pass yet.

I mentioned President Joe Biden earlier in this chapter. His political career began as a young senator at twenty-nine and his first presidential run was at age forty-six, but he did not obtain his goal for another thirty-two years, when he was seventy-right. Still, he didn't give up. He worked toward his vision.

Think about your vision. What resides in your heart that is more important than your own life? Write your dreams (Hab 2:2). Continue to pray about the vision God placed in your heart (Hab 2:3). Assess your associations, and adjust where needed.

I try to live in a way that I will not need a tombstone. I will not need anyone to announce that "here lies Wale Akinosun". I hope that my name and my works will live in the hearts of people. The legacy I strive to leave is that of my character.

The word *character* originates from the Hebrew word meaning *statue* (rigidity). Statues do not change. Come rain or shine, they hold the same posture. Statues were chiseled into shape, just as God shapes us (Isa 64:8), the potter and the clay.

When the scriptures tell us to die daily to ourselves (1 Cor 15:31), it is to rid ourselves of things that are hiding the perfect image God created. A sculptor cannot design and build a perfect image that is always moving. When going through challenges, stand still and fight the battle. Let God give you character. Stand still and see the salvation of the Lord (Exod 14:13). Let God build your character. Based on your character, people can predict how you will respond or what you will do in your absence. This is all part of manning your gate.

VII. Diehard Commitment

In each of the five times "it came to pass in the day(s)" is used in scripture, it denotes impending trouble, followed by deliverance and a happy ending (Ruth 1:1; Gen. 14:1; Esther 1:1; Isa. 7:1; Jer. 1:3).

The Book of Ruth is a story of love, devotion, and it is the story of a Moabite woman who forsakes her pagan heritage in order to cling to the people of Israel and to the God of Israel. Because of her faithfulness in a time of national faithlessness, God rewards her by giving her a new husband, a son, and a privileged position in the lineage of David and Christ.

14 Then they lifted up their voices
and wept again; and Orpah kissed her
mother-in-law, but Ruth clung to her.

15 And she said, "Look, your sister-in-law
has gone back to her people and to her
gods; return after your sister-in-law."

16 But Ruth said: "Entreat me not
to leave you, or to turn back from
following after you; for wherever you
go, I will go; and wherever you lodge,
I will lodge; your people shall be my
people, and your God, my God.

17 Where you die, I will die, and
there will I be buried. The Lord do

so to me, and more also, if anything
but death parts you and me."

(Ruth 1:14–17)

Not much is said about Naomi, except that she loved and cared for Ruth. Naomi's life is a powerful witness to the reality of God. Ruth was drawn to her, and to the God that she worshipped.

In the succeeding months and years, God led the young Moabite widow to a man named Boaz, whom she eventually married. Together, they had Obed, and as a result, she became the great-grandmother of David and an ancestor in the line of the Messiah (Ruth 4:13; 16–17).

During the time of Judges, there was disobedience, idolatry, and violence. Today, we have our own share of those things. Yet, even in times of crises and despair, there are people who follow God and through whom God works. Ruth was committed to herself, to others, and to God. This commitment was unshakable, and built upon a strong foundation.

Commitment

Commitment shows up in your life through what you do and where you devote your time. It reveals two things: reasons and results. Reasons do not count. Results matter. There may be reasons why you do not live your dreams, but no one can argue with results. You judge a tree by the fruit it bears (Luke 6:44), and not what it might talk, think, or wish.

Everyone is committed to something. It is how we participate in life. What are you committed to? Mediocrity or excellence, loyalty or disloyalty? Everyone's commitments produce results in their life. Whenever I'm asked how I'm doing, my favorite response is, "I'm doing well, but there is room for improvement."

How do you spend your time? What are you committed to? Are you satisfied with your lot in life? Do you want to make more money, live healthier, stop bad habits, or improve relationships? What commitments have you made to make those things happen? What you do determines your results.

You can make a commitment today, and go for it. When Naomi made a commitment, she followed through. She did not make excuses.

No Excuse is Acceptable

Excuses are easy to make. We all make them. Some are small, such as when you trip or spill something and look to cast the blame on another, even if no one was near you. Others are more serious, and can cause a decline in personal growth, such as excuses of procrastination. People are often afraid of commitments because it means they have to deliver. Have you ever asked someone to commit to something and they replied, "I will try." That is an escape clause. It is a very polite, "No." Perhaps they readily and quickly agreed, but when it came time to perform the task needed, "something came up" or "I was just so busy..."

You either do or you do not.

Commitment means that no excuse is acceptable, even if it is inconvenient or you later decide you don't want to do something. It is imperative that you honor commitments that you make to yourself, to others, and to God, with no excuses.

Breaking commitments gradually erodes your self-esteem and weakens your faith in yourself. It develops weak relationships with people because they know you won't keep your word. It ruins your reputation because it teaches people that they cannot rely on you to do what you say.

Do the things you say you will do. Do not even speak words until you're willing to stand behind them. What would your life look like if you decided to keep your word?

17 Thus God, determining to show more abundantly to the heirs of promise the immutability of His counsel, confirmed it by an oath,

18 that by two immutable things, in which it is impossible for God to lie,

(Heb 6:17–18a)

Start Today

First, commit yourself to live in the present. Carpe diem is a Latin aphorism, usually translated as "seize the day". This often repeated phrase is taken from book one of the Roman poet Horace's work *Odes*. So, why do I bring this up? Because it's a good motto. There's value in such a thing. Stop looking back and replaying what has already happened. At the same time, stop looking too far in the future worrying. *Carpe diem*. Even the scriptures have a verse for that.

Sufficient for the day is its own trouble.

(Matt 6:34b)

When you keep commitments, especially to yourself, you begin to get better results in life. You will probably not be able to keep 100% of those commitments, but you can continuously work toward them. Start with a commitment to go into business, or to change habits that work against you, or whatever is in your heart.

You will soon see that you are overcoming self-destructive behaviors and redesigning relationships. You are seizing the day and manning your gates.

Make it a Priority

If you thought your chances of reaching your destination were the same as your luggage, you would never get on an airplane. We all know of someone who has lost their luggage or had it delayed for a significant period of time. Maybe it even happened to you. But what about when you board the plane and take your seat? The reason you will get to where you paid to go is because the airline has made it a priority. There is a story of a person who boarded a wrong flight when going to attend a wedding.

They were trying to fly to Ontario, California, but had boarded a flight to Ontario, Canada. Because the airline made delivering passengers to the destination a priority, they announced the destination several times. The person soon discovered their error. Perhaps they did not feel it a priority to double check their destination before boarding the plane. Don't make that mistake.

How do you do that? Keep reading.

Set Smart Goals

Have you heard of SMART goals? SMART is an acronym for: specific, measurable, attainable, realistic, and timely. It is good to be ambitious, but also good to be realistic. I decided to increase my exercise regime recently. I have gym equipment in my basement that I do not visit. There is a flowerpot on my treadmill, blooming beautifully. I decided to start doing pushups daily; I began with ten sets, twice daily, and now I am at twenty sets. If I had started out at fifty, I would not be there. Working up and starting small was a realistic and achievable goal.

Additionally, I decided that I was going to increase my giving every year, as a mark that God is increasing me. It also helps to build my faith in God's word and promises.

Now may He who supplies seed to the sower, and bread for food, supply and multiply the seed you have sown and increase the fruits of your righteousness.

(2 Cor 9:10)

Now, it does not bother me or make my heart faint. I call it my annual increase; the same way that I expect to get an increase at work.

Accountability and Creativity

Changes sometimes cannot happen without encouragement. They also won't happen without accountability. But what about creativity? How does that come into play? Let me explain about each of these. For accountability, you need friends who won't let you off the hook and will only tolerate the best from you. When you tell people that you are a Christian, they will help you be a Christian.

Commit to being creative about your initiative so that you can challenge yourself. Whenever you come against difficulty, it is okay to wait on God, but be sure that you're not simply hiding your lack of commitment to yourself. Stretch yourself and use your imagination. The more you do it, the easier it will become. This creativity may actually help you to discover a new way to stay accountable.

Your actions and the way that you represent yourself have a lasting effect on others. Your deeds are critical, and also set an example for those around you. The people who are committed to customers, family, neighbors, and friends make the greatest impact in life.

Be kindly affectionate to one another
with brotherly love, in honor giving
preference to one another.

(Rom 12:10)

Hunger and Thirst

Commitment is being hungry. There is no questioning Ruth's hunger and thirst. God responds to this type of commitment. The scriptures share examples of this. Are you committed? Are you acting as Ruth did?

Ask of Me, and I will give You The nations for Your inheritance, And the ends of the earth for Your possession.

(Ps 2:8)

And he who overcomes, and keeps My works until the end, to him I will give power over the nations.

(Rev 2:26)

The outcome is not the same for the person who commits a little and then stops. Face your disappointments and refuse to be discouraged until life gives your desire up to you. Nothing can resist a person with that kind of commitment. Continue to work. Stand firm and man your gates. Keep your eye focused on God.

Make a commitment to stand up for yourself as a channel for God to work through you in all things. Run your own race. Do not compare yourself to others.

When they cast you down, and you say, 'Exaltation will come!' Then He will save the humble person.

(Job 22:29)

When the enemy comes in like a flood, the Spirit of the Lord will lift up a standard against him.

(Isa 59:19b)

Don't expect people to understand you or agree with you because oftentimes they will not. It is also important to realize that you know that you will not always win. That's life. Do not become discouraged and tempted to go back to what you used to do or slip into habits that do not serve you or God. Do not make excuses to not finish. When something happens, own it, learn from it, stand up, and keep pressing toward your mark.

Encourage yourself, and at the same time, do not put yourself in positions that make you fail on your commitments. Refer to the scriptures for reinforcement.

17 If that is the case, our God whom we serve is able to deliver us from the burning fiery furnace, and He will deliver us from your hand, O king.

18 But if not, let it be known to you, O king, that we do not serve your gods, nor will we worship the gold image which you have set up.

(Dan 3:17–18)

God is Spirit, and those who worship
Him must worship in spirit and truth.

(John 4:24)

5 If any of you lacks wisdom, let him ask of
God, who gives to all liberally and without
reproach, and it will be given to him.

6 But let him ask in faith, with no doubting,
for he who doubts is like a wave of the
sea driven and tossed by the wind.

7 For let not that man suppose that he
will receive anything from the Lord;

8 he is a double-minded man,
unstable in all his ways.

(James 1:5–8)

I pray for you as you decide to make a diehard commitment.

What now?

As you have turned these pages, you've learned about the importance of your actions. You've learned that your commitment and focus are critical. It's time to put each of these components together, looking at past events. With these tools given, these stories from the Bible, and the real-life lessons included, you are now prepared to man your gates. You are able to help others man their gates. You are able to keep your temple impenetrable.

As you move forward, as you stand your ground, protecting that which is most sacred and precious, remember to kneel often in prayer. Call to your Father in heaven, look to Him in strength, and seek Him in times of sorrow or burden.

Stand strong like David. Be resolute like Ruth. Remember Nehemiah and Ezra. Man your gates.

www.ingramcontent.com/pod-product-compliance
Lightning Source LLC
LaVergne TN
LVHW020650100826
845148LV00012B/2409

9781737094975